7/89

SO-BOK-218

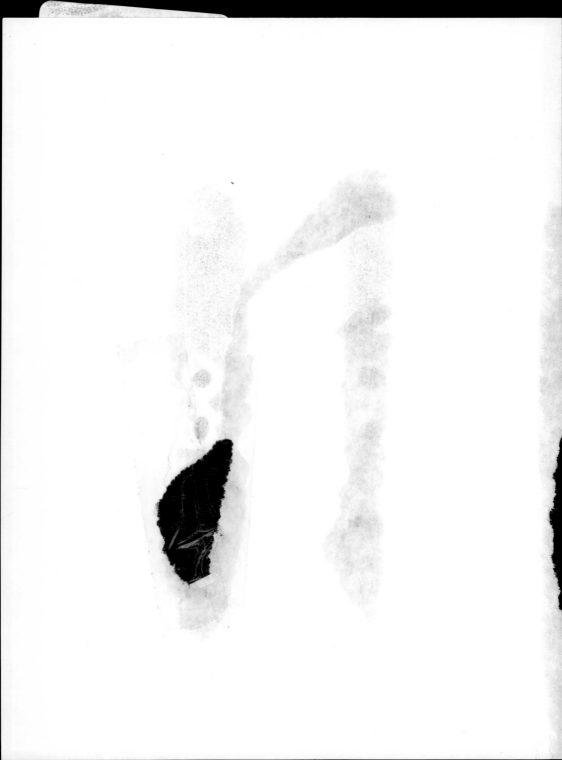

SOMALIA

SOMALIA

DEARDRE GODBEER

ACKNOWLEDGEMENTS

The Author and Publishers are grateful to the following organizations and individuals for permission to reproduce copyright illustrations in this book:

Action Aid; Geoscience Features Picture Library; Hutchison Photo Library; C. J. Martin; Oxfam; Vivant Univers; Visnews; World Vision International.

The Author would also like to thank Professor B. W. Andrzejewski, Paul Holmes, Dr Ioan Lewis, R. J. McNeff, C. J. Martin and the Women's Corona Society for their encouragement and help in the preparation of this book.

J
916.773   12.95
1. Somalia
I. Title

Chelsea House Publishers.
95 Madison Avenue, New York, NY 10016
345 Whitney Avenue, New Haven, CT 05510
5068-B West Chester Pike, Edgemont, PA 19028

Contents

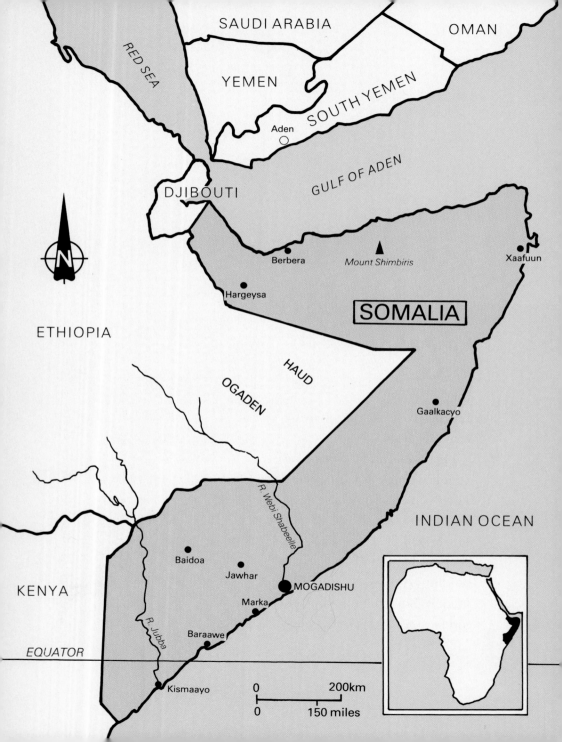

The Horn of Africa

The Somali Democratic Republic lies in the Horn of Africa beside the Indian Ocean. The Horn of Africa is the protruding tip on the east coast of the continent of Africa. Somalia, as it was first called by the Italians who colonized the area in the nineteenth century, looks rather like an elongated figure seven. It covers some 638,000 square kilometres (246,000 square miles). The Gulf of Aden lies to the north of Somalia; to the south is Kenya and to the west are Ethiopia and part of Kenya. In the northwest is Djibouti which is an independent country, although its people are part of the same race as the Somalis.

There are also three areas of land which Somalia continues to claim as its own. These are the Haud, the Ogaden and areas on the border with Kenya. The Haud and the Ogaden are the traditional grazing lands of the Somalis; they border on Ethiopia to the north and west. These areas are the homeland of a million and a half Somalis. Wars for control of these regions have occurred periodically since the fourteenth century.

7

Goats nibbling the sparse grass of the Somali scrubland. Its arid, sandy soil supports only scattered grass clumps and stunted bushes and trees

In the late nineteenth century, following a successful war against the Italians (who were trying to set up a vast empire in East Africa), and their Somali allies, Ethiopia claimed the Haud and Ogaden areas as its own. The Somalis, however, have never accepted this claim, and the dispute over the land continues. Similar problems have arisen over the border between Somalia and Kenya, because the British backed the Kenyans in their claims to what had traditionally been Somali territory.

An aerial view of the country shows vast areas of semi-arid scrubland, desert and sparse vegetation. The only things which

8

stand out are the acacia trees and the *mundille* (mud houses), thatched with mats, in small clearings. In some areas the soil looks red; in others it is quite black. The black soil is valuable because it is fertile and can be used for growing crops.

Stretching inland for a distance of 100 kilometres (60 miles) along the entire Indian Ocean coast of Somalia is an area of grassland. Trees and succulent shrubs can be found on the tip of the Horn of Africa, and there is open woodland over a large area of northern Somalia about 200 kilometres (125 miles) inland from the Gulf of Aden. However, when the rains fail (roughly every seven years), the land becomes an arid desert.

A vast area of semi-arid scrubland extends beyond the coastal grass in the areas behind Gaalkacyo and Hobyo towards the Ogaden in the centre of the country. To the south, beyond the

A group of thatched mud houses, called *mundile*

The fertile green banks of the River Jubba. Maize, rice, sesame, wheat and cotton are cultivated in the river valley

capital Mogadishu, thicker open woodland between the rivers Jubba and Webi Shabeelle provides a home for much of Somalia's varied wildlife.

The Jubba and the Shabeelle are Somalia's two most important rivers. They flow from Ethiopia right across Somalia towards the Indian Ocean. The land on either side of the rivers is fertile and cultivated. Crops such as bananas, sesame and wheat are grown there. Streets and hotels in the capital city are named after the Jubba and the Shabeelle, because they are extremely important to the Somali people as a means of irrigating the land and supporting daily life.

The mountains begin in the northwestern part of Somalia on the Ethiopian border and continue right across to the Horn. The highest mountain in the country is Mount Shimbiris which is 2,416 metres (7,927 feet) high.

Further south is an area, known as the Haud, where the Somalis have traditionally grazed their camel herds and cattle. The Haud lies between the area once known as "British Somaliland" and the Ethiopian border. This area receives less rainfall than the mountains and it also has a warmer climate.

Nearer the equator, around the southern town of Kismaayo, the climate is hotter. The temperature in Somalia varies from 30 to 40 degrees Celsius (85 to 105 degrees Fahrenheit); the atmosphere is also very humid. The sea does, however, serve to cool the towns nearer the coast where the climate is pleasant and healthy as a result.

Half of Somalia is inhabited by nomads—people who wander from place to place in search of grazing for their animals. The desert and scrubland are ideal for their way of life. The Somali nomads are known for their proud and handsome bearing. They are tall, with strong bones and fine white teeth. The nomads have very little in the way of material possessions—their camels are their treasure.

The farmers in the south of the country may not resemble the cattle-raising nomads from the north but, as they produce the crops, they are also very important to the economy of the country. They often have quite dark skins because they work in the fields all day.

The Somalis' skin may vary from a golden chocolate colour to a very dark brown, but there are some Somalis with almost white skin. It is not uncommon to see three brothers whose skin colour varies from coffee to chocolate to black. This is because of the intermarriage in the past of the Somalis with Arabs, or with Italian, French or British colonial families.

Many Somali women are very beautiful and have long, straight, black hair. They walk with grace, swinging their hips like majestic camels. Some Somali men in the past have written poems about their girlfriends in which they liken them to a camel. This may sound strange, but the camel is a very honoured member of Somali society, as it is a source of meat for food, milk for drink, transport for moving house, and also shade from the sun. The nomad in the desert would be quite lost without his camel. The camels wear bells which are carved from wood by the nomads of the bush. When the bells are tied around the camels' necks, they make a distinctive sound. It is quite striking to hear the camels as they cross silently over the desert with only the *chunk chunk* of the bells to indicate where they are. In Somalia it is customary for the men to look after the camels whilst the women look after the goats and sheep.

There are many different groups of people in Somalia. Some, like the ancestors of the Darod tribe who form the largest tribe, originally came from Saudi Arabia. Others came from other parts of Africa. The names of some of the tribes are: Marrehans, Rahanwein, Habr Awal, Dulbahante, Essa and Ishaq. In the past, tribal loyalties were very strong in Somalia. This meant that people achieved high positions in society through their family connections rather than through their ability to do a job well.

12

Somali men digging watering holes for their camels. According to custom, men look after the camels, while goats and sheep are the women's responsibility

Nowadays, however, whether they come from the north or the south of the country, everyone is equal in the Somali Democratic Republic and a person is judged by what he or she contributes to society rather than by where he or she was born.

There are five main cities in Somalia, of which Mogadishu, the capital, is the largest. In this city, with its mixture of grand Arab-style buildings, banks, hotels and schools, the old twelfth-century mosque and modern parliament buildings rub shoulders with the huge Italian-built cathedral and triumphal

13

arch. The many new hotels offer all modern comforts; but not far away a labyrinth of tiny alleys and high walls with slit windows houses the poorer quarters where hundreds of small traders eke out a living and where children run happily in and out of doors. Still further out lies the Arab part of the city, where Somali and Arab families live in tin-roofed shacks. In the evening many adults sit outside nodding peacefully, while their children snuggle around them. It is a moving and colourful contrast to the formal, tree-lined avenues just around the corner, where many foreign embassies are housed.

Hargeysa, the second largest city in Somalia, used to be the capital in the days of British administration. It is an orderly and well-kept town. Here, nomads are a more frequent sight than in Mogadishu; and traditional Somali dress is more common than the westernized suits and dresses of the south. The pace of life is

The coastline near the capital city of Mogadishu

A view of Baraawe, a southern port famous for its leather goods markets. Its inhabitants speak a dialect better understood by the neighbouring Kenyans than by fellow Somalis

less hectic, too, although many business and political negotiations are conducted in Hargeysa. As a result, the city is a convenient place to test the political temperature of the nomads and the religious leaders, as well as a market centre for the traders who then sell their wares in Berbera in the north.

Berbera is a very important port for Somalia, because it is here that the trade in livestock takes place. Like most Somali cities and towns, it has all the basic municipal facilities, such as schools, hospitals, post offices and mosques. The inhabitants of Berbera have a reputation of being very cosmopolitan, because of the city's strong links with Aden and the Saudi Arabian ports.

In the south of the country lies the town of Baraawe, whose

15

industrious population does a thriving trade in leather goods. People here speak a dialect more comprehensible to their Kenyan neighbours than to fellow Somalis. An Arab influence from the past can be deduced from the lighter shades of the inhabitants' skin colour.

Kismaayo, the major town of southern Somalia, lies on the equator close to the Kenyan border. People on both sides of the border have much in common: they speak very similar languages; and there is a great deal of commercial and cultural exchange between them.

Modern Somalia (or, to give it its full name, the Somali Democratic Republic) is a country where ethnic and cultural differences do not pose a serious political problem, as they do in many other African countries. Over the decades, the Somalis have learned to coexist peacefully within their society, which accommodates different lifestyles and branches of Islam with equal ease.

Somali History

THE TRIBAL AND COLONIAL PAST

The earliest remaining evidence of civilization in Somalia are finds of Graeco-Roman origin, such as beads, an alabaster vase, fragments of jars and pieces of earthenware pottery found at Salwain, on the northern coast. Fragments of soapstone and blue-glazed pottery, thought to be from the ancient empire of Parthia in southwest Asia, have been discovered at Xaafuun. These fragments, together with burial platforms and large circles of stones in burial places, are thought to date from between the first century BC and the first century AD. However, Somali history can be traced back even earlier than this.

In Biblical times, fragrant myrrh and frankincense were brought from Somalia to the temples of Egypt. There were many Egyptian expeditions to Somalia and, although the details of these are not recorded, the fact of their taking place is recorded on the tombs of Egyptian officials. The first recorded expedition to Somalia was made in 2400 BC and concerned the

17

Incense sellers in a Hargeysa street. As early as 2400BC the Egyptians organized expeditions to the part of Africa that is now Somalia to bring back the precious myrrh and frankincense

trade in incense and ivory. Much later, in 1470 BC, Queen Hatshepsut of Egypt sent a trade mission to Somalia. The details of this are engraved on the temple walls at Thebes.

The people of Somalia are said to be descendants of Ham, one of the sons of Noah. Some time before the birth of Christ, a southern Arabian tribe known as the Gallas, crossed the Red Sea and intermarried with the original inhabitants in the Horn of Africa. In the early seventh century there was a further migration of Arabs from across the Red Sea. These people

18

married into the already mixed race of Gallas and Africans, and present-day Somalis are thought to be their descendants.

The oldest known Somali tribes are the Dir Somali, the Darods and the Isaq; many branches and sub-tribes stem from these groups. Other early inhabitants of the land included the Hawiye, and also the Midgans, who were outcast tribes—"the hewers of wood and the drawers of water". They received protection from the larger tribes in exchange for their labour. The Midgans were also hunters and leatherworkers. They made prayer mats and religious amulets as well as shoes, wallets, straps and other useful articles. If a Midgan woman married a man from another tribe, the offspring were known as Tomal. These people were ironworkers and made knives, swords, spears and arrow-heads. The Yibir were another early tribe in Somalia. They spoke a different language from the other tribes and traded in magic, telling fortunes and casting spells.

These tribes were nomadic and inhabited the northeastern area of Somalia. At the same time there were some settlements along the coastal region and southern borders. For example, Mogadishu, the capital of present-day Somalia, is thought to be over one thousand years old. Its name is probably derived from the time when the Persians ruled there and means the "Seat of the Shah". Arabs and Persians had established a string of coastal settlements in Somalia in the centuries following the birth of the Islamic religion. Arab and Persian colonizers had established themselves in considerable numbers in Mogadishu during the tenth century and it was from Mogadishu that the expansion of

19

the Islamic religion and Arab trading routes throughout northern Africa began.

During the first part of the tenth century, Mogadishu was a divided city. Descendants of the Persians lived on one side of the wall, and the Arabs and Somalis lived on the other. The Somalis were the rulers. There are still houses and mosques in Somalia which date back to this period. Pottery from China, Persia and Arabia has also been found, indicating that Somalia was trading with these countries. Similarly, coins portraying twenty-three different rulers have been discovered. It is thought that Somalia minted its own coins from 1300 to 1700.

By the fourteenth century, Muslim Arabs had converted most Somalis to Islam. Under the leadership of Sa'ad ad-Din, the Somali Muslims called for a holy war against the Christians in

The Arab quarter in Mogadishu. In the tenth century Mogadishu became a divided city in which people of Persian origin lived separated by a wall from the Arabs and the Somalis

Ethiopia. At first they were successful but later, in 1415, the Muslims were defeated and the Emperor of Ethiopia pursued and killed Sa'ad ad-Din. The Ethiopian Negus Yeshaq wrote songs celebrating this victory over the Somali Muslims and this is the first time the name "Somali" appears in ancient records in Ethiopia.

There followed a century of peace until Imam Ahmed Ibrahim al Ghazi fought the Ethiopians and won many victories. The Portuguese were also a major power in the Red Sea area at this time. They sought to expand their own empire and trade routes, and the Ethiopians turned to them for help. Imam Ahmed was finally defeated in 1542 by Emperor Galawdewos of Ethiopia.

The Darod tribe were also fighting at this time and were in possession of Mait, an ancient port in the north of Somalia. The Darods formed the large Midjerteine Sultanate in the years 1540-1560 and came to control most of the northeast coast of Somalia. Gradually, the Darods began to migrate south, pushing before them the Gallas who were also being forced out of their traditional lands by the arrival of new groups of Arab settlers from across the Red Sea. Many Gallas finally settled in the Ogaden region on the present-day border between Somalia and Ethiopia. The Gallas, together with the Ethiopian Christians, were naturally opposed to the Darods who had seized their land.

It is from this time that the tales of Wilwal have been passed down from generation to generation. Wilwal Garad Farah Hersi came from Jijiga in the Ogaden. He was a famous chieftain who was always able to outwit his enemies with the help of his wife Ebla. Even today he is looked upon as an example of courage and tenacity; the traditional stories of his exploits are well known to Somali children.

During the seventeenth century, the city of Mogadishu was invaded by the Somali Darods, and the Gallas were driven south of the River Jubba. The Darods fought the Gallas and eventually reached the port of Marka. By the eighteenth century, Somalia had grown virtually to its present-day boundaries.

In the 1840s the Darods moved on to the River Shabeelle where they were halted by tribes known as the Rahanwein and the Oromo. These tribes were absorbed into the Darod tribe and thus protected from other enemy groups to the west.

In the early twentieth century, the Darods continued to move southwards down the coast of Somalia and succeeded in overcoming various tribes in the west and the southeast of the country. Many of the hunters of these areas became serfs to the Darods. Gradually the Gallas and Oromos, too, became absorbed into the Darod tribe and this ended the great migration of the Darods which had been going on for nine hundred years. The Darods had literally fought their way into the area now known as Somalia and settled there. They also took the semi-desert plains of northern Kenya and established their people there.

Meanwhile, three major European powers had also become interested in occupying Somali territory as it became an

The Mogadishu cathedral. It was built by the Italians, who out of the three colonial powers—Italy, Great Britain and France— had the strongest cultural and economic impact on Somalia

important trade route to the Middle East. These countries were Britain, Italy and France. Gradually, by a series of agreements with the rulers of Somalia (the sultans), the country was divided up between these European powers. The sultans had a great deal of power among their own people but they were also anxious to keep the peace, maintain their trading rights, and protect their cattle. In order to do this, they were prepared to reach agreement with almost anyone who offered friendship and protection.

In 1825 a British brig—the *Mary Anne*—foundered on the

Somali coast and the crew were attacked by Somalis. However, the governor of Zeila (a port on the northern coast) agreed to protect the crew because he thought that by supporting the British he would strengthen his own position. His attitude angered the British government and the British then blockaded the Somali coast for eight years and demanded that the Somalis pay a heavy fine.

Later, a commercial treaty was signed between the Somalis and the British East Africa Company. By this time, the British had established a presence in Aden, across the Red Sea in Arabia. It became important for the British to trade with the Somalis as they needed meat for their soldiers. The meat was shipped from Berbera in northern Somalia—the main port for trade with Aden. In time, the British took control of the port and, in 1887, the northern area of the country became the British Somaliland Protectorate. As a result, the Somalis were taught the English language, and the British legal and political systems were introduced.

At about this time, the Italians signed treaties with the sultans of Midjerteine and Obbia in the centre of Somalia. They, too, were interested in gaining Somali ports as trading bases. In 1889, the Italians signed a treaty of perpetual peace and friendship with the Ethiopian emperor Menelik. The Italians hoped to overrun all the countries of East Africa in order to form a large empire with Ethiopia. They claimed that the 1889 agreement had given them a protectorate in Ethiopia. Because Menelik rejected this claim, the Italians turned against the

Ethiopians and used Somali soldiers to fight them. However, the Italians and Somalis were defeated at the battle of Adawa in 1896. The Ethiopians were quick to draw up boundary lines and, in 1897, the Italians agreed to terms which involved giving away parts of Somalia to Ethiopia.

Towards the end of the nineteenth century, the Sultan of Zanzibar (the large island off the East African coast), who also owned the Somali coastal ports, had been persuaded to accept British management of his land. This enabled the British to protect the coastline of the mainland against other powers.

In 1905, the British leased the Benadir ports (which include Baraawe, Marka and Mogadishu) to the Italians. In the same year the British persuaded the Sultan of Zanzibar to give Italy absolute possession of the Somali ports in return for payment of £144,000 sterling and also leased to them land near Kismaayo in the far south of Somalia. The Italians eventually took control of this area, and consequently the Somalis in the south were taught the Italian language, and were ruled by Italian legal and political systems. This area became known as Italian Somaliland. It extended south from the boundary with the British Protectorate as far as the River Jubba.

In 1908, the British administration induced the Ethiopian emperor Menelik to extend the British boundary. The Italians were not happy about this and subsequently the frontier was extended from Dolo on the River Jubba to the River Shabeelle. This arrangement gave the Italians an additional 50,000 square kilometres (31,000 square miles) of Somali territory, for which

A stretch of the coastline of southern Somalia along which are lined the Benadir ports—Mogadishu, Marka and Baraawe

they paid the Ethiopian emperor three million lire. This area included Baidoa, the granary of Somalia.

By then, the French had also claimed 13,672 square kilometres (8,492 square miles) of land in the northern region of Somalia, around Djibouti. This added to the division and colonization of Somalia, so that the whole country was now ruled by European powers.

Many of the Somali Muslim leaders were unhappy about the colonization of their country. One mullah (Islamic theologian), named Muhammad bin Abdullah, decided to do something about it. In 1898, he built a mosque and a teaching centre which followed the strictest Muslim principles. Warning his people that the Christians were dominating their country, he urged them to

26

join him in fighting a *jihad,* or holy war, against the Christians. By 1899 he had an army of three thousand men. More than twenty years of fighting followed and the "Mad Mullah", as he was called by the British, held off the British forces in a fanatical and sometimes cruel war. He also terrorized other Somali tribes who refused to submit and fight to the death for Islam. The long war continued until Muhammad bin Abdullah was finally defeated by the British in 1920.

During this period, the Italians were quietly building their empire and developing a highly efficient agricultural system producing, among other things, cotton, sugar, and bananas. The British, too, were making modest headway in agriculture and education.

Then came the Second World War (1939-1945), which prevented both the Italians and the British from undertaking further colonization. During the Second World War, Italian and British forces fought each other in Somaliland. In August 1940, the Italians captured British Somaliland and added it to their empire. Seven months later, the British regained the Protectorate, and Somalia and the Ogaden were occupied by the Allies, including Britain. The Italians gave in so easily that the British were taken by surprise and had barely enough officers available to administer their new territories.

THE STRUGGLE FOR INDEPENDENCE
Resentment of the colonists had been growing in Somalia. In 1943, an organization known as the Somali Youth Club was

27

founded in Mogadishu. A number of Somali police officers, trained by the British, also became involved in the Youth Club. By 1947, the club had changed its name to the Somali Youth League, and there were 25,000 members. This Somali Youth League developed into a well-organized, nationalist party which was later to play a decisive role in the making of modern Somalia.

It was the Somali Youth League which, in 1947, finally brought to a head the divisions between the British-influenced Somalis in the north and the Italian-influenced Somalis in the south. In spite of the differences in language, law and politics, the Somali Youth League got together a government which the British felt could finally bring the country forward to independence. The Somali government was formed in 1956; and in 1960 Somalia was granted independence. The first president after independence was Aden Abdullah Osman and the first prime minister was Abdi Rashid Ali Shermarke.

There were many problems in the early days because the leading Somalis were nearly all from one tribe (the Darods) who had mostly lived in the south under Italian rule. Another tribe (the Isaq) did not like this and there were quarrels among politicians of different tribal allegiance. Many people felt that the Darods held all the opportunities. Things became even more difficult when Mogadishu, a southern town, was made the capital of the country.

There were different ideas about the legal and political systems of the two areas and about whether the official language of the country should be English or Italian. It was three years

28

before the government was able to bring the Somalis of the north and the south together in a unified Democratic Republic of Somalia. (Djibouti, hower, remained in French hands. Even when it eventually became independent, it did not reunite with the rest of Somalia.)

Nine years after independence a revolution took place in which Abdi Rashid Ali Shermarke, who had become president in 1967, was murdered whilst on a mercy mission to famine areas. He was shot by one of his own guards. The motive behind the murder was partly political and partly to do with powerful tribal jealousies.

After the revolution in 1969, General Muhammad Siyad Barre took power. He said at the time that he had stepped in to bring order to the country. With the help of the Soviet advisers

Children celebrating the anniversary of the 1969 Revolution, which brought General Muhammad Siyad Barre to power

introduced to Somalia by the first government, he formed a new government and made Somalia a communist state.

Loudspeakers on all street corners broadcast programmes on communist ideals. Huge placards featuring President Siyad Barre were everywhere and every house had to display a portrait of him. Everyone was proclaimed equal and had to work for his or her living. Large teaching centres were built to teach communism to the people. The main centre was called Hallane, after a Somali who had died rescuing the Somali flag during one the many wars with Ethiopia. Artists were told they could not paint any pictures which did not explain communist thinking and praise the workers.

President Siyad Barre's government was called the Supreme Revolutionary Council and consisted of the Regional Revolutionary Council and the District Revolutionary Council. In addition, there was a Committee of Secretaries, consisting of fourteen young civil servants. These men were chosen not for tribal reasons but for their ability, and they were responsible for the day-to-day running of the country.

Six years after the revolution, there were many self-help programmes; the largest of all was the programme to teach the nomads to read and write. Somalia is a vast country and about thirty thousand secondary school students and teachers were sent into the bush to teach literacy and principles of communism to their fellow countrymen. The sultans were no longer in power; they had become *Nabadons,* "Peacemakers", and had to explain the new teachings to the nomads. The bush people could

A sultan listening to his tribesmen

trust their sultan but few of them knew anything about Siyad Barre.

At the end of the 1970s, just as things were beginning to go well, and the nomads were learning to read and write, a terrible famine spread. The students had to give up teaching the nomads and turn to helping the starving people in huge refugee camps. Many nomads were sent to the south coast to be trained as fishermen, while others were sent to become farmers along the riverbanks in the south. The nomads, who were very proud of

31

their own way of life, did not like this at all and some escaped. Tribes were split up and people were separated from their families, so that large family groups could not become too powerful.

In 1976 the Supreme Revolutionary Council, which had governed Somalia since 1969, was dissolved and its powers were transferred to the newly formed Somali Socialist Revolutionary Party—the only political party allowed to exist in Somalia. General Muhammad Siyad Barre remained in charge of the government.

In 1977 the Soviet advisers were given one day to get out of Somalia. This was because the Soviet Union had switched its support from Somalia to Ethiopia; and President Siyad Barre was worried that the Ethiopians, backed by the Soviet Union and Cuba, would try to take over his country. The president then went abroad and asked for aid from several Western countries. At the time he was not very successful, but later the United States promised aid, and Britain, Egypt, Italy and Saudi Arabia also helped Somalia on its way to economic development without Soviet aid.

WAR, FAMINE AND REFUGEES
The Somali Democratic Republic today faces many problems. Some of these problems are a result of colonial rule, when Somali territory was lost to other nations; others are a result of natural disasters.

The Somali flag, created on independence in 1960, is a five-pointed white star on a blue background. The five points of the star represent areas of land which have been taken from Somalia by foreign powers.

The areas represented by the star are the northern frontier district of Kenya, which the British gave away; the port of Djibouti, which was taken by the French; the northern area of Somalia, which was ruled by Britain; the Italian region in the centre and the southern coastlands of Somalia; and the Ogaden and Haud area which the Somalis claim has been stolen by the Ethiopians.

Land is very precious to the Somali people who naturally feel very bitter about the loss of large parts of their territory. The United Nations Organization was asked to help Somalia resolve its land disputes but did not want to become involved in this difficult problem. As a result, the only thing the Somalis could do was to go to war and try to win back the land themselves.

Ethiopia became a communist state in 1974 when the Emperor Haile Selassie was deposed. The Ethiopians had been fighting the Somalis in the Ogaden for a long time. The Ethiopians used Soviet-built Mig aircraft to bomb the Somalis who lived in the Ogaden on the borders between the two countries. The Somali men in the Ogaden fought back but their women and children had to escape. At one time, napalm bombs were used and many Somalis were badly burnt and in need of specialist medical care. Cuba and the USSR had armed the Ethiopians against the Ogaden Somalis.

Since President Siyad Barre had expelled all Soviet advisers

33

The Somali flag, adopted on independence in 1969. The five points of the star represent the five regions which Somalia claims have been taken away from it by foreign powers

from Somalia in 1977 there was tension between the two countries at that time. Somalia had no alternative but to seek help from America and other Western countries. The Ethiopian communists wanted to expand towards Somalia, but the Americans did not want communist domination of the Indian Ocean because of its strategic ports and gateway to the Saudi Arabian oilfields. In 1980 Somalia agreed that America could use the military base at Berbera and have access to ports and airports in return for military and financial aid. In this way, the simple border dispute between Ethiopia and Somalia soon became a matter in which the superpowers were involved.

To make things worse, there was also a war going on in Eritrea (a province in northern Ethiopia) and many Somalis had supported the Eritrean people against the Ethiopians. So the Somalis were fighting Ethiopia on two fronts: in the Ogaden area on the border; and in Eritrea, which is peopled by Somalis, near Djibouti. The war in Eritrea caused thousands of refugees to flee into neighbouring Djibouti and northern Somalia. They were joined by Ethiopians loyal to Haile Selassie, the former emperor of Ethiopia, who were now in disfavour with the Ethiopian government.

To complicate matters still further, there were also many Somalis who disagreed with the politics of President Siyad Barre. These people, who were mostly from the Midjerteine and Isaq tribes, formed a large army in the Ogaden area. They called

President Muhammad Siyad Barre. Throughout his rule there have been outbreaks of tribal and religious conflicts in Somalia

themselves the Democratic Front for the Salvation of Somalia. This Somali opposition army then infiltrated refugee camps in Somalia in order to increase opposition to President Siyad Barre. There was mutiny and rioting in 1983. Many opposition leaders were shot, while others were imprisoned and tortured. An amnesty was declared by the president in 1984, but only two hundred people took advantage of it.

The Somalis opposing the president then tried to gain international recognition for their cause by hijacking a Somali aircraft in 1984. This finally focused world attention on Somalia's problems. The President regained some power and enlisted all Somali men between the ages of eighteen and forty into the army for two years. In this way he re-educated the people in his particular brand of socialism and protected his army from infiltration by the opposition. In December 1984, there was another one-party election and President Siyad Barre was again elected as the country's leader.

In February 1986, President Siyad Barre went to Djibouti where he had important talks with President Mengistu of Ethiopia and President Arap Moi of Kenya. They agreed to set up a committee to find ways of solving their problems.

In addition to the ravages of war, Somalia has suffered a tremendous natural disaster. Between 1978 and 1981, a devastating drought affected the whole of northeast Africa. The Somali nomads lost thousands of cattle, camels, goats and donkeys whose carcasses lay strewn across the barren scrubland. Some thousands of people struggled on in the blazing heat, gasping for water, until they arrived exhausted at the refugee camps. The number of people affected reached nearly two million according to government reports, although these figures are said to have been exaggerated.

In 1980, President Siyad Barre asked for international aid. Seventeen relief organizations from all over the world went to the aid of the starving people, most of whom were women and children. Among these were International Christian Relief, Action Aid, Save the Children, World Vision and Oxfam. Some camps had as many as 700,000 refugees. International Christian Relief, caring for one of the largest camps, reported:

"There was a repulsive sickly smell, there were no wells, no toilets. The people were getting hookworms. Sixty per cent of the refugees had tuberculosis; others had scabies, malaria, lung infections and dysentery. There was at first no sanitation, food, water or medicine. These people had been through unspeakable ordeals and were only just alive."

On arrival at a refugee camp, children were weighed, measured and issued with supplementary food allowances if they were under a certain weight. Pregnant women and nursing mothers were also given supplementary food. (A mother in Somalia usually breastfeeds her baby for two whole years.) The sick and the elderly were also given extra milk, cereals, food made from carrots, fruit juice and high-protein biscuits. Feeding took place twice a day. A nurse would start her day at 5.45 a.m. and finish perhaps at 9.00 p.m. There was help from Somali

37

Mothers and their children in a refugee camp near Hargeysa queue for extra rations of milky gruel

nursing auxiliaries, but it was very hard work indeed. Other helpers included Somali teachers and students who taught the refugees to read and write.

It was necessary to provide food, water, medical supplies, cooking utensils, fuel, lamps, tents, lighting, toilets, vehicles and supplies for maintenance, as well as blackboards, chalks, exercise books and pencils for the teachers.

In 1981, the rains came but they brought about yet another disaster because there was immense flooding. Huts made of grass with cardboard roofs were soon swept away and thousands of square canvas mats had to be provided to cover the thornwood frames. The flooding also ruined some of the poorly stored grain and flour supplied by foreign aid. Goods which had been lying in the sun were soon damp and inedible.

In 1985, relief aid was still necessary because some people were still sick with diseases caused by malnutrition. The plight of the starving people of Africa was made known to people throughout the world. Organizations such as Band Aid, started by pop star Bob Geldof, and Sport Aid combined show business and artistic skills with sports marathons to collect vast sums of money. However, all the money in the world cannot resolve the problems of refugees when severe drought and war are combined. The most valuable type of aid is that which teaches people to help themselves by using modern irrigation and farming methods so that future generations will never have to face such devastation. Unhappily, in 1987 there was a further drought.

The People of Somalia

Nomads inhabit half of Somalia and are traditionally considered to be the aristocrats of Somali society. They wander from place to place in search of grazing for their animals, setting up temporary enclosures with portable huts. The huts have walls of thorn brush and roofs made of mats which are tied on securely with hand-made string. Inside each hut, known as an *aqal*, a long mat hangs parallel to the wall to form a corridor along which a visitor must walk before entering the main part of the hut. Cooking-pots and clothes are hung on nails around the wall, as are narrow beds made of string woven across a wooden base. The hut is therefore uncluttered, clean and neat. The women sweep their homes with long brooms. Everyone sits on finely-woven mats on the floor or on low divans.

A large fire is built in the centre of the enclosure at night and there is always someone on guard. The fire must be stoked to keep away lions, hyenas or leopards which may prowl around and attack the sheep or goats penned inside the enclosure with

A camel owned by a nomad family, loaded with everything needed to set up house at their next stop in the semi-desert

the camels. The boys guarding the camels sleep in the open on a large communal mat within the enclosure.

These enclosures are not permanent because the nomads are always moving on in search of new grazing land. When there has been little rainfall and grass is scarce, Somali nomads walk for days across the parched land. The men lead, followed by the camels loaded with mats and twigs for building the huts. The women walk behind, sometimes carrying water in jars made of leather and bound with wooden bands. Wood has to be gathered in the new grazing area to make the fences for the enclosure and

41

also to make charcoal for the fire; all this is women's work. The women also cook the meals and grind the maize.

The men wear a long white cloth wound around the waist and draped over the shoulder. Their hair may be combed right out and padded with hair supplied by the women of the family. It is then covered with mud. Sometimes *ghee* (clarified butter) is smeared over the head to keep away insects. Sometimes the hair is dyed red with henna. The nomad traditionally carries a stick and kettle and perhaps some Muslim prayer beads. He also carries a pillow made of wood. Other than this, he has very little in the way of material possessions.

A Somali woman wears a cloth which she winds around herself and ties across her right shoulder, like an Indian sari. This dress is called a *guntina*. A married woman wears a short headscarf, usually black, to tie her hair back tidily. Over this comes a flowing *garbusar*, or long scarf, which covers her head and arms.

One great feature of nomadic life is sitting around the fire in the evenings. When it is dark, the black sky shows hundreds and hundreds of bright stars. There are no skyscrapers, no tall trees, no hills—just bare desert and a vast starry sky above.

The sky has intrigued the Somalis for generations. As a result, they have become famous as astrologers and astronomers. One famous Somali, Musa Galal, has written a book all about Somali astronomy and astrology. It is called *The Terminology and Practice of Somali Weather Lore, Astronomy and Astrology* and was published in 1969 in Mogadishu.

Somalis traditionally consult an astrologer before arranging a marriage or a special journey, to see if the day they have chosen is forecast as being a lucky or an unlucky one. If it is predicted as an unlucky day, the marriage or journey is postponed until a more favourable time.

Each month the moon is absent from sight for one or two nights. The Somalis call this the *Dubbad* period. Any boy born at this time is considered to be "blessed". He is never allowed to shave his head because his hair is said to be a blessed crown. This means that he is a special person with a blessing on his head, and so his hair is holy.

The Somalis have amazing memories and some can quote the whole *Quran*—the Muslim holy book—by heart. Until quite recently Somalis relied entirely on their memory to recount history or to tell important news. As there was no written language, they were very gifted at recalling things accurately. Many older Somalis can speak five languages or more, because of the many nations who have either governed them or traded with them in the past.

One of the greatest assets of the Somali nomads is their talent for composing poetry. They also compose fine songs, called *gabays* often dealing with political or historical events. Sometimes Somalis address love songs to their womenfolk or their camels! Often, they accompany their songs with instruments such as a lute or drums. Occasionally, the music is played on a flute which sounds strangely haunting in the still of the desert night.

In the bush the Somalis practise traditional medicine. For example, they use a special root which, when chewed, staunches bleeding. If someone breaks a limb they can make good splints and bind the limb until it heals. One treatment consists of applying burning charcoal twigs to areas of the body where there is pain. This acts on the nerve in much the same way as acupuncture and stops the pain. Many Somalis have scars on their chest or back where they have undergone this treatment. Muscular pain can be eased by standing on the patient and seemingly walking over them. The Somalis know exactly where to place the feet to relax the patient's muscles and relieve the pain.

The ancestors of today's Somali farmers originally lived in the southern river areas. Over the years, they mingled with the nomadic tribes which migrated south and intermarried with the local established farming people.

The life of the farmer is more stable than that of the nomad who is constantly on the move to find fresh grazing lands for his camels, cattle, goats and sheep. The farmer builds a fenced enclosure, or kraal, with several thatched houses within it. The women and girls are kept busy with the domestic chores— weaving mats, pounding maize, attending to the babies and washing clothes—but they go into the fields to till the land as well. The work is long and arduous and the tools they use are very simple. A family may be occupied for many months and then earn just enough from the grain they can sell to the government to enable them to live at subsistence level.

The Somali farmer may keep a few chickens but in the main he is employed in producing food crops for his family to eat and for sale. In the south, crops such as maize, sorghum, bananas and other fruit are grown. In the northern uplands, wheat, barley, potatoes, cabbage, tomatoes, onions, sweet peppers, fruit and even a little coffee are cultivated. Farmers use a donkey and cart to take their wares to market. It is from their colourful market stalls that the vegetables and fruit are sold to the townspeople.

In the past, the main occupations of Somali farmers were date-growing and the cultivation of the aromatic incense trees. Now, other crops have gradually been introduced by the government in conjunction with the international relief agencies. Education in the prevention of soil erosion, provision of seed banks, training in horticultural techniques and the choice of seeds for different soil types, as well as small-scale irrigation schemes, are some of the projects now under way.

Many Somalis now live in the towns and cities, particularly since famine in recent years has driven people towards places where food and water are more readily available. Life in the city differs a great deal from the nomadic way of life.

An average businessman will be at his office by 8.30 a.m. There will be a break for coffee at 10.00 a.m. This involves going to a coffee-shop with friends. Whereas in other parts of the world a coffee break may last half an hour at most, Somalis often extend their coffee break until lunchtime. The coffee-shops are, in fact, an extension of the office; it is here that much of the real business is done. Politics are discussed, interviews given, sums of

A village woman pounding maize outside her hut. Somali women work hard: apart from housework and bringing up their children they also help the men in the fields

money exchanged. However, no women visit the Somali coffee-shops; they are uniquely the province of the men. Much of the Somali businessmen's work is done outside the office. They work hard at establishing contacts and communication through the coffee-shop system.

After lunch, there is usually an afternoon siesta until 4.30 p.m. when another visit to the office or shop may be made. As the evening cools into sudden darkness at around 6.00 p.m., the whole town comes alive. The women put on pretty dresses and walk out in style. The elegance of the Somali women, with their exquisite gold jewellery, would cause a flutter of admiration in any society in the world.

Somali townswomen are early risers, getting up at about 6.00 a.m. to prepare breakfast. First the maize must be pounded to make a porridge-like meal, then the coffee, too, must be ground. Somali women do not eat with their husbands. They serve their menfolk first and then eat their own food separately with their children.

Lengths of brilliantly coloured cloth on sale at a market

Once the children have left for school, the Somali housewife goes to market or to the small Arab and Indian stores to buy rice, sugar and tea. The market consists of hundreds of small stalls, with colourful displays of potatoes, tomatoes, cucumbers, onions, garlic and *ghee*. Baked bread rolls can also be bought from the market. One section of the market houses the charcoal dealers, who do good business since most Somali women cook on charcoal ranges. There are also separate markets for fish and meat.

Many little stores display brightly coloured lengths of material made especially for the *guntina*, the traditional dress of Somali women. The cloth stores are always a centre of gossip as the women help each other choose the right material for this or that occasion. As there are no ready-made clothes on sale, the women must go to a tailor to have them made. The tailors provide a wonderful selection of modern and traditional dress patterns from which the customers can choose the style they want.

It is quite common for Somali women to visit one another in the morning. The visitor is offered coffee or an orange drink and there is much laughter and chatter and pretence at shyness. The visit rarely lasts longer than half an hour. This is considered just the right length of time to enjoy a visit, but not long enough to intrude. A Somali woman may visit several homes in a morning. At each house she listens to all the gossip and the political news, for her husband relies on her to keep him informed. There are no gossip columns in Somali newspapers, but everyone knows what is going on.

Once the shopping has been done and the daily visits made, the Somali housewife returns home to supervise the cleaning. Usually a young niece or close relative does the basic housework and helps with the cooking, whilst the mistress of the house organizes the work and gives a hand where necessary. Many poorer Somali women work as paid servants in the homes of those who are more prosperous, but they are often treated almost as one of the family by their employers. Somalis are very democratic by nature and there is no class structure in Somalia of the kind known in Western countries.

The traditional picture of the Somali woman as a person who spends all her time looking after her home and family is changing, however, and nowadays many women in the towns attend university or college. These women are much more liberated than the older generation. Many young women take degrees in law or medicine and go on to take an active part in the running of the country.

Industry, Crafts and Agriculture

Throughout the colonial period, and in the first years of independence, the Somali economy relied on the export of banana crops—sold mainly to Italy—for much of its foreign income. The Italians were also involved in the establishment of a sugar cane plantation and alcohol distilleries at Jawhar.

There is, as yet, little industry in Somalia, but things are slowly improving. Periods of famine have spurred the government to build up the fishing industry, which now processes quantities of tuna fish and shark for European markets. In 1984, the Italians built Somalia's first pharmaceutical plant; and there is now an edible-oil processing plant near Jawhar, which produces and packages cooking oil from various locally grown seeds.

There has been some prospecting for petroleum and uranium by American and West German companies: However, no mineral resources have so far been found in Somalia that would increase the pace of the country's industrialization. Such industry and trade as there is depends to a large extent on

50

foreign aid, and it is clear that this will be required for many years to come.

Most industries in Somalia are agriculturally based, using animal products (mainly hides) or plants (such as cotton or tree bark). Much of the production takes place in small workshops, where artisans patiently practise their time- and labour-consuming crafts.

There are several traditional crafts in Somalia. Tanning and leatherwork have been known since the early days when the Midgans made crude sandals, amulets, vessels for water and milk and cowhide beds. During the colonial period, the Italians taught the Somalis more modern techniques of leatherwork. In

A leatherbound copy of the *Quran*. The tooled designs show the skill of the old craftsmen

the nomad community, tribal craftsmen still make simple leather sandals from camel skins, as well as cowhide couches which are suspended by loops on the walls of the house during the daytime.

There are now large tanneries and leather factories in Mogadishu and Baraawe, where sandals and handbags with fringed fronts are made. Goatskins are exported to foreign glove manufacturers and there are local markets where tanned hides are sold to craftsmen. Beautiful coats are made from

Ripe cotton seeds have burst open to reveal the soft white fluff, ready for picking. It will be cleaned, spun and woven into cloth

A weaver at his loom. Homemade cloth is often dyed and printed before it is taken to the market

leopard skins, while cheetah-skin sandals are popular with women in the towns. Intricate tooled designs on leatherbound old copies of the *Quran* show the accomplishment of the old Somali master craftsmen.

Cotton is grown in the Benadir region of Somalia—the coastal strip around Mogadishu. The soft fluff surrounding the cotton seeds is first cleaned and then spun and woven into lengths of cloth according to traditional methods. In the local weavers' quarters, little narrow streets lead into yards where the freshly woven and dyed cotton cloth is pegged out to dry in the sun. As in the earlier times, the weavers squat before large wooden looms, and they work the same ancient patterns; the posture and

53

the simple machinery have changed only very little over the centuries.

The string mats used in Somalia are made from the fibres of tree bark which is pounded and chewed by women to soften it. Most of the wooden furniture is produced by local carpenters.

Other local products are made from ivory and tortoiseshell, derived from relatively rare, often endangered, species of animals, and are therefore quite expensive. Pipes and candlesticks made out of the mineral meerschaum (a silicate of magnesium also known as sepiolite) are popular with tourists, who scour local markets for interesting souvenirs. Beadwork of very fine blue and white beads plaited together, necklaces made from shells or real amber found on the coast, and small carvings can all be bought from the market stalls.

For centuries, Somalia has been the leading exporter of frankincense, a type of aromatic resin used to make incense. Myrrh and other fragrant plants used in the production of incense and perfumes are also grown here.

At one time, farming in Somalia was restricted to the fertile areas along the banks of the rivers Shabeelle and Jubba. However, since the revolution in 1969, many agricultural projects have been established and new areas have been cultivated. When Somalia's communist government first came to power, people were ordered onto trucks and driven to work in the fields. Many of the photographs in the newspapers shortly after the revolution showed the Somalis working together to improve their country's agriculture. Traditionally, the farming

54

A woman weaving a decorative mat. These mats are used at home to sit on, or sold at the nearest town market

profession was despised in Somalia and the nomads, wandering in search of grazing for their animals, were considered to be far more noble than the settled farmers in the south of the country. Nowadays, however, three-quarters of the employed population are engaged in farming.

Almost immediately after the revolution, about 570 farm cooperatives and intensive work programmes were set up. The idea behind the farm cooperatives was that several farmers joined together and shared a stated amount of land between them. For example, about ten families shared tools and worked

55

together to plough, sow and reap the harvest. In this way, the farmers shared the expenses and helped one another.

At first the Somalis worked enthusiastically on these cooperatives. Soon, however, problems began to arise. Because of the very damp climate in Somalia, farming equipment began to rust and wear out. Many ploughs and farm tools lay abandoned and unused. It was impossible to obtain spare parts and the country did not possess the necessary skills to make new parts and tools. Moreover, the Somalis themselves became disillusioned with the cooperative farming system. Despite their hard work, they had nothing to pass on to their children because they did not own the land they farmed. The profits made from crops were taken by the state and used to buy seeds and equipment for further development.

Soon ill feeling began to grow amongst the people. There were even incidents where farmers burnt their crops rather than allow the state to take the profits. These farmers were denounced as traitors and shot as an example to others. This frightened the people for a while, but the resentment continued to grow. More recently, however, the government has changed its policy and now allows limited private enterprise. People are permitted to own a certain amount of land and property and to keep some profit for themselves. This has given Somali farmers an incentive to work harder and, as a result, agricultural production has improved.

In addition, international aid programmes have spent a lot of time and money helping both the countless refugees and the people of Somalia to grow their own food on cooperative farms. They have established farming areas far away from the traditional places in the south of the country. One group, Action Aid, specializes in teaching horticulture to Somali women.

The Somalis' traditional methods of farming are very old-fashioned. Their simple tools are made for the individual farmer with a small area of land. Now, heavy equipment is being supplied and distributed by the Agricultural Development Corporation. Between 1982 and 1986, the Somali government allocated fifty per cent of its budget to agriculture. Because Somalia is such a dry country, it is particularly important to improve irrigation. One such project will make it possible for the Somalis to grow rice and cotton in a previously barren area of the country.

New roads are also being built which will make it easier to transport food from the farming areas to the towns. The World Bank is financing a project to build a road between Jawhar, the centre of a thriving agricultural area, and Buulobarde. The money must also be found from foreign aid to pay for spare parts for farm machinery, for new machinery that is needed, and for fertilizers.

Certain areas of Somalia use flooded land agriculture which relies on seasonal watercourses. This means that during the rainy season certain low-lying areas are flooded to leave arable land which can then be cultivated. By this means, areas of the country which were not previously used for agriculture are now being turned into arable land. Durrha (a cereal crop which is a

A banana plantation in Somalia. In the first years after independence, the import of bananas to Italy kept the country's economy afloat. Today, bananas are the second largest export

type of sorghum), maize, cotton, sesame and groundnuts are all grown in these areas.

There are banana plantations covering some 70,000 hectares (173,000 acres) in the traditional agricultural areas in the south of Somalia, along the Jubba and Shabeelle rivers. Bananas are Somalia's second largest export after livestock. The Somalis also grow sorghum, maize, fruit and cotton in this important area of the country.

The livestock industry is now thriving in Somalia. The Livestock Development Agency has set up branches throughout the country to encourage proper treatment, veterinary care and feeding. The breeding and care of these animals constitutes a most important part of the Somali economy. In the past, black-headed Berbera sheep were reared in their thousands for export to Saudi Arabia. Since the Saudi government placed an embargo on imports from Somalia in 1983, the Somali economy has suffered greatly. However, livestock is now being exported to Egypt and North Yemen. Gradually, after the terrible famine of the early 1980s, cattle, sheep and goats are being reared and trade is at last healthy again. Somali goats are comparatively easy to rear as they feed on almost anything, even rubbish. Goats can be seen everywhere, even in the streets of Mogadishu. The goat is a popular source of food; its meat is very tender if cooked

A flock of black-headed Berbera sheep. Many are exported to Egypt and North Yemen

Cattle drinking the clear water of the River Shabeelle

properly on a charcoal fire, and its milk is very nourishing.

Eggs from free-range chickens can be bought in the local market. The chickens are rather scraggy—mostly because they are poorly fed—but this area of farming could be developed. The milk produced in Somalia is treated in a modern processing plant and bottled for use in the cities.

In the past, Somalia has had to import food grains, edible oils and medicines. The USA, Italy and the United Kingdom still supply some of these, but it is hoped that the time will come when Somalia will be fully self-supporting. Given the necessary aid from foreign friends, the Somalis will succeed in making their country independent in this way.

The Muslim Factor — Religion, Law and Customs

Most Somalis follow the Islamic religion. All Muslims, regardless of which country they come from, see themselves as belonging to the same nation of believers; and Somalia has joined the Arab League (an association of Arab Muslim states) to show its conformity to Muslim ideals. This is both a religious union and a political one.

The "Five Pillars of Islam" set out the duties of Muslims all over the world. The first Pillar of Islam is the *shahada*, or declaration of faith, in which a Muslim must proclaim: "There is no God but Allah and Muhammad is His Prophet." Secondly, all Muslims must pray five times a day. When praying, they must face towards Mecca, the Muslim holy city in Saudi Arabia. Muslims do not need to go to the mosque (the Muslim place of worship) to pray. They carry a prayer mat with them and unroll it wherever they happen to be at the appointed time. Friday is the Muslim holy day, and on Fridays all the shops and businesses in Somalia are closed.

The third Pillar of Islam is known as *zakat*, and this involves giving a certain percentage of one's income to the poor. Fourthly, as a sign of self-denial and devotion to God, Muslims must neither eat nor drink during daylight hours for one whole month each year. This month is known as *Ramadan*. Finally, everyone who is able to do so must make a pilgrimage to Mecca at least once during his or her lifetime. This pilgrimage is known as the *hajj*. A man who has made the pilgrimage is known as a *haji* and a woman as a *hajia*.

Muslims use prayer beads—these are strings of either ninety-nine or thirty-three beads, the smaller type of which is commonly used by women. They recite one of the ninety-nine names for Allah over each bead. There is a joke among Muslims that there were originally one hundred names for Allah—but the last name is hidden in the camel's hump and he is not telling anyone what it is! The ninety-nine names for Allah can be found in the *Quran*, the Muslim holy book, and each name describes one of the attributes of God.

Saints are an ancient tradition in Somali Islamic culture. There are many saints and their tombs can be seen dotted all over the landscape. Muslim saints are recognized, after death, for their godly lives and for acts of piety, kindness and mercy to those in need. The burial place of a saint is venerated and sometimes a small mosque is built over the spot. The widow of a saint will spend much time at his grave, replacing the stones and caring for it with great devotion and respect. The power of the saint is said to be strongest at the saint's graveside every year in the month when he died, and people come in their hundreds to chant and pray. Dervishes, or holy men who have taken the vow of poverty, come to these areas to teach the people the *Quran*. A holy man usually stays for one month at the tomb of his special saint and from there he goes out to the people to beg for food and to give blessings. (A holy man in Islam has no property or goods; he abandons everything in order to follow Allah.)

Sometimes a person will tear a piece of cloth from his own clothes and attach it to the railings around the saint's tomb, as a promise that if the saint grants his request he will perform some good deed. The good deed is often in the form of an offering to the guardian of the shrine. This might be anything from a pot of *ghee* (clarified butter) from a poor person to a sum of money from a rich one.

Some very famous saints have been credited with miracles such as healings, rain-making and the bringing of children to childless couples.

There was once a holy man named Sheikh Mur Muhammad ("Sheikh" is the name Somalis give to an important holy man) from Hargeysa in the northern region. His people came to him in a severe drought and asked him to pray for rain. The Sheikh prayed. Within the hour clouds appeared, lightning flashed, thunder roared and enough rain fell for all their needs.

Another story is told of Sheikh Ali Gure, who died almost two hundred years ago. Sheikh Ali Gure was old and half blind, and only three attendants travelled with him. During one journey, he told his attendants to set him down on the ground and then to go

Boys from the Quranic school. The wooden slats bear the versicles from the Holy Book, which they learn by rote and chant during the lessons

and rest under a tree, and he would call them when he needed them. After some time they went to look for him but he was nowhere to be seen. Eventually he reappeared. "Where have you been?" they asked. "A sailing ship with some Muslims on board got into difficulties at sea," he replied. "One of the Muslims prayed to God and said 'Please mend our damaged ship, through the blessing of your saints.' This cry reached my ears. By the power of God I was transported there and I placed a board over the hole in the ship." According to the story, it was by the same power that the Sheikh returned to the place where his followers were waiting for him.

Tradition has it that Sheikh Ali Maye was able to give people the gift of foreign languages. The story is told of how he asked that a small orphan boy named Yusuf should be brought to him. At first the people brought the wrong boy. The Sheikh sent him away. The people searched and found another orphan boy called Yusuf from the same tribe. They brought him to the Sheikh. At once, the Sheikh rushed towards him, picked him up and, as he was a very small boy, kissed him on both cheeks.

He took little Yusuf and led him to school. For one day, Yusuf learnt the *Quran* by repeating it after the Sheikh. Next day, Sheikh Ali Maye asked little Yusuf to read the *Quran* to the class. "Father," said Yusuf, "I don't know anything, how can I?" "God willing, you will know," said the Sheikh. Then he spat on Yusuf and slapped him on top of his head, and suddenly the little boy could speak Arabic fluently and read the *Quran* aloud.

There are countless such legends concerning the powers of various saints; these tales, and rituals associated with the cults of individual saints, enrich Somali culture while also strengthening its links with the international Muslim community.

Just as the Christian religion has several different groups, such as Protestants and Roman Catholics, so there are divisions within the Islamic faith. These groups differ from each other in their views on how strictly people should abide by their religion.

One of the most important Islamic groups in Somalia are the

Sufi, who are deeply spiritual people. There are three groups of Sufi Muslims in Somalia—the Qadiriya, the Salihiya and the Ahmediya. The Qadiriya, who have been established in Somalia since the fourteenth century, have a great respect for the Muslim saints. They emphasize the spiritual side of life and generally tend not to involve themselves in modern problems. The Salihiya are a much more fanatical sect. The Ahmediya, whose form of Islam was introduced into Somalia at the end of the nineteenth century, concentrate on teaching the *Quran* (the sacred book of Islam) and the *Hadith* (the body of traditions and legends about the Prophet Muhammad and his followers).

Other Islamic groups in Somalia today include the Muslim Brotherhood and the Salafi. The Muslim Brotherhood believe that people must return to God. They teach about the different sects in Islam and want to encourage religious tolerance between these sects. They encourage intensive prayers, the reciting of the *Quran* and the learning of the *Hadith*. Qualities such as bravery, generosity and endurance in hardship are praised, while weaknesses such as inconsistency, idleness, talkativeness, lack of discipline and tribal rivalry are considered to be contrary to Islamic teaching. The Muslim Brotherhood do not agree with being loyal to just one tribe, but feel that all believers should be part of one international family.

The Salafi Muslims are mainly young graduates in Islamic theology from Saudi Arabian universities. They follow the Islamic religion very strictly and believe that people should not pray to saints or seek help from anyone but Allah (God).

66

Since the revolution there has been a certain amount of conflict between various Islamic groups and the Somali state. The socialist government of Siyad Barre does not encourage organized religion. For their part, the religious groups see some of the reforms introduced by the government as being contrary to the teachings of Islam.

For example, when the government set up a committee to decide which script to use when writing the Somali language for the first time, it was decided to use the Roman script—the same script which is used in writing English. This angered many strict Muslims who wanted to use the Arabic script. This is because the *Quran* is written in Arabic and Muslims consider Arabic to be the language of God.

More conflict occurred in the early 1970s, when some Sufis formed a group called "The House of Saints". Their main aim was to create the opportunity for discussion amongst different Muslim groups. However, this led to their criticizing the government and to one of the Sufi leaders, Sheikh Omar Yusuf of Haraf, being imprisoned near Hargeysa. Sheikh Omar Yusuf was a Qadiriya who gained many followers. He was kept in prison until September 1978, just a month before his death, and his followers became known as the Sufi Reformers.

The Sufi Reformers realize that the modern educated Somali does not agree with some of their teachings. Their aim is to change the inner soul of each person. They want people to follow Islamic teachings and Islamic law to the letter in all aspects of everyday life. One of their leaders, Sheikh Nur Ali Alow, was

67

imprisoned for years without trial because he wanted the Somali government to abide by the *Sharia* (traditional Islamic law).

In 1975, the government passed a law which said that men and women had equal shares in inheritance. This is quite contrary to Islamic teaching, which states that men must have the greater share. The Muslim elders (the *ulama*) confronted Siyad Barre's government on this point. At an open committee they questioned his legal right to change Islamic law. This led to the execution of ten of the leading *ulama* and the imprisonment of over two thousand men in Mogadishu. Even those who cared little for their religion were outraged at this public demonstration of state interference and, in defiance, there were many recruits to Muslim organizations.

The government allows the Muslims to practise their faith only as long as it does not conflict with any government interests. Sometimes work takes precedence over prayer. Most Muslims in Somalia want to revive Islam in a modern way. Divisions amongst the Muslim groups cause weakness, and those who really care about their religion hope that with wise, persistent, committed and realistic leaders, unity will prevail among the believers.

Somali laws were originally founded on Muslim *Sharia* law, as laid down in the *Quran*. However, now that Somalia has become a socialist state, other laws have been introduced. There are 114 articles of Somali law which cover many aspects of life such as freedom of religion, freedom of speech, education, electoral rights, the right to work, the equality of citizens, the right to own land and property, and child welfare.

The judicial system is made up of the Supreme Court, the Military Supreme Court and the National Security Court. The Supreme Court is presided over by civilian judges who decide issues concerning civil rights, financial affairs and the administering of punishment. The National Security Court is responsible for cases involving crimes against the state. There are courts of appeal in Mogadishu and Hargeysa and eight regional courts which are divided into two sections, general and assize. There are also eighty-four district courts with two sections, civil and criminal. The civil court decides all matters where *Sharia* law is concerned. The criminal court deals with minor offences for which the punishment may be up to three years' imprisonment or a fine.

Religious magistrates, known as *Qadis*, deal mainly with marriage and divorce. Marriage in Somalia used to be arranged by the parents, but nowadays young Somalis make their own choice. However, certain traditional customs are still followed. The groom's family pays *yarad* (a gift to the bride's family) which usually consists of cattle or money. The bride's family makes a return gift after the marriage, which usually includes the *aros* (bridal house). The main legal part of the ceremony is the signing of a document in which the woman agrees on *maher*—a sum of money which will be hers in the event of the couple divorcing at some later stage.

The actual wedding ceremony, in which the *Qadi* recites

A religious magistrate, known as a *Qadi*. Since the Revolution the *Qadis* have been confined to family law, marrying and divorcing people, while other matters have been taken over by the state

prayers and quotations from the *Quran,* is quite simple. There is usually a small celebration at the time of the marriage. However, the main feasting and dancing can continue for days; and it is customary for beggars and holy men to seek alms at this time. Nowadays, large festivities have given way to group marriages in the town hall, in order to spare some of the expense.

Divorce is very common in Somalia. It is only necessary for a man to repeat three times in front of witnesses "I divorce you" and the divorce is an accomplished fact. However, many husbands stop at the second pronouncement and give their wives another chance. After a man has divorced his wife he must

70

keep himself free to care for her for at least three months and she may continue to live in their home. This is in case she is pregnant, for no Somali man would abandon his wife if she were in this condition. The divorce is officially legalized in a paper signed by the *Qadi*. The woman is then paid her *maher* and this money allows her to return to her family home with honour.

A divorced woman who wishes to remarry her first husband may not do so until she has first married and divorced another man. After a second divorce she may return to the first husband and remarry him according to *Sharia* law.

The most common reason for divorce is when a woman has become too old to have children. The husband then looks for a younger wife in order to continue the family line. It is customary to give the first wife gold bangles when she is left for a younger

A Muslim burial ground near Afgoi. Small piles of stones mark the graves, in contrast to the Western bronze and marble

bride, so that there is no suggestion that the first wife is not loved by her husband. The first wives are not unhappy and abandoned but become part of the extended family.

The death of a Somali is marked by family mourning. As it is very hot in Somalia, the body is buried on the day of death. Most Muslim burials are simple religious ceremonies and the tombs are often without a headstone. Sometimes just a pile of stones marks the place.

Death in Islam is a joyous occasion; a widow is not expected to show grief in public. During the period of mourning she wears bright colours to symbolize the fact that her husband has gone to paradise. The official colour of mourning in Somalia is white.

Poets and Storytellers

A great Somali talent is the ability to compose poetry. Until quite recently poetry was never written down, although it was used from the very earliest days as a means of communication. When important messages had to be conveyed to the people, the men would gather under a tree and the elders and wise men would discuss the matter. When a decision had been reached it would be passed on to the local poet, who would compose a poem which the Somalis called a *gabaye*. The contents of these poems might affect a whole community and might bring peace or war to an area. Indeed, poetry was sometimes used to bring about political changes.

A poet was a very important person in the community. After he had created his poem, he would recite it only once. He was not paid but was greatly honoured. If the message needed to be conveyed to others, this was done by poetry reciters who had to be word perfect. As they chanted the poem, the reciters were not permitted to act or show any facial expression, nor were they

73

allowed to stress words or sentences. The reciters had incredible memories—the average length of a *gabaye* was about one hundred lines. The poet's name was also recited on every occasion.

Poems were written about local history, current affairs, well-known personalities of the time and the customs of Somali society. It was a great honour to take a message from one community to another. Once the reciter had agreed to take a message, he was honour-bound to deliver it to the person or persons concerned and it had to be recited exactly as it had been told to him.

The need for this beautiful oral poetry has decreased since the nomads have been taught to read and write. Tape recorders and transistor radios, which are now widely used in the bush, have also put a stop to this special Somali practice. Sadly, this may cause these talents and cultural treasures to die out. However, there are some Somalis today who collect all the oral poems they can find and turn them into classical Somali literature. These books are written in the Somali language—this, in itself, is a great achievement since the form of spelling used was agreed upon only in 1972.

There was much talk and disagreement about whether the language should be written in Roman or Arabic script, the latter being a familiar part of Islamic culture and therefore known to many Somalis. Eventually, it was decided to use Roman script. Since then, the Somalis have been very busy writing school textbooks, teachers' manuals, public records, street signs, documents, certificates, licences, money, stamps, price lists and menus all in their own Somali language.

Today, even complicated mathematical and technical text-books are written in Roman script in the Somali language. Words have been invented to convey modern technical terms. Perhaps it is because of the *gabayes* and the long tradition of memorizing them that Somalis concentrate hard and are receptive to new ideas and to progress.

The Somalis have recently begun writing their own plays which they perform regularly at the National Theatre in Mogadishu. The National Theatre was built for Somalia by the Chinese in 1969. There are also theatres in many of the larger towns throughout Somalia. This interest in writing plays developed in the mid-1950s. During the period of colonization, the British had taught drama as part of the school curriculum. The school plays gave rise to theatrical productions in village halls. Similarly, the Italians had produced local Somali plays which ultimately developed into the Somali theatre. Today, the National Theatre and national radio stations perform Somali plays. Some Somali playwrights have had their work translated abroad. One such famous poet, playwright and broadcaster is Hassan Sheikh Mumin.

Wildlife

The wild animals of Somalia are highly prized, not so much as tourist attractions but as the constant companions of the nomads. The leopard is the Somali symbol, and official government stamps and parade flags show one leopard on each side of the Somali flag.

The leopard's beautiful hide (tawny-yellow, with black spots) is much coveted by hunters. However, the government now allows very few to be hunted because of the danger of their becoming extinct. The leopard can be found in northern Somalia and along the northeastern coast and also in the far south near the River Jubba.

Elephants roam along the banks of the Jubba and Shabeelle rivers and in the far south of the country, bordering on Kenya. The African elephant is almost four metres (over eleven feet) high at the shoulder and weighs six tonnes. It has a large head with huge flapping ears, a long flexible trunk and single incisor teeth elongated to form tusks on either side of the upper jaw.

A leopard slinking towards a drinking hole. Its black-spotted coat is in great demand by hunters but hunting is restricted

Somali elephants are valuable for their ivory tusks and for this reason they are carefully watched and protected from poachers.

Gazelles can be seen in many areas of the country. They live in small family groups of up to seven and they feed on durrha grass on the plains. They also eat the leaves of umbrella-shaped acacia trees. Gazelles move from area to area according to the time of year and the plants in leaf. There are five different types of these gentle creatures. The *dibatag*, or Clarke's gazelle, has a long neck and is greyish-fawn in colour, with a white streak on each side of its face ending in a whitish ring around each eye. Only the males have horns which curve backwards in the lower third and then forwards and slightly out. The long-necked gerenuk gazelle is similar in many ways but has a light chestnut-coloured coat.

These two varieties can be found on the Somali side of the Haud region and in the eastern coastal strip. Other types of gazelle in Somalia are the Soemmering, the Speke and the Pelzeln's gazelles. These have smaller antlers than the *Dibatag* and can also be found along the entire coastal strip from the north of Somalia down to Mogadishu.

In the south, towards Kismaayo, the beautiful giraffe can be seen. In ancient times, the gift of a giraffe between rulers was a symbol of peace and friendship. Unfortunately, in some countries the giraffe has been wiped out because its hide is used to make many articles. The Somalis make sandals and water buckets from giraffe hide.

Five different types of dik-dik (a type of small antelope) roam

A pair of giraffes, their heads lost amidst the foliage

the north of Somalia and the areas around the rivers Jubba and Shabeelle. These are very tiny and exceptionally beautiful animals. They stand thirty to forty centimetres (twelve to sixteen inches) at the shoulder. Their coat is soft, coloured grey to reddish-brown, and white to grey on the underparts. Only the males have horns, short and stout at the base, ringed and grooved and often partly hidden in a tuft of hair on the top of the head. The tail is a mere stump; and there is a puffy hairy muzzle and longish snout. The dik-dik makes a shrill whistling sound which annoys hunters because it alerts other animals to the danger. It can be heard to make a sound like *dik-dik* or *zik-zik* as it browses—hence the name.

The dik-dik is shy and elusive, but if startled it leaps stiff-legged, rather like a hare, in a zig-zag course. Its trembling delicate babies are a soft cinnamon colour and stand roughly twelve centimetres (five inches) high at birth. The emblem of the Somali police is two dik-dik horns mounted on a silver badge.

In the south of Somalia, near the Shabeelle River area, another type of antelope may be seen. This is the kudu which has spiralled white-tipped horns and a pretty striped coat. The lesser kudu has a scanty mane and is yellow-grey with white stripes on the flanks, a white crescent on the throat, another white crescent on the chest, and white spots on the cheeks and nose. The greater kudu has a thick upright mane extending to the back and a throat fringe. Its coat is reddish-fawn, becoming blue-grey in the males. It, too, has white stripes on the flanks and spirally twisted horns.

Lesser kudu—an antelope with a pretty striped coat and a white crescent on both throat and chest

Crocodiles can be seen in the rivers, while along the river banks live the oryx, with their black and white face markings and long, slender scimitar horns. Hartebeest and common ringed waterbuck also live in this area, together with hippopotamuses and African buffaloes.

Several types of zebra are native to Somalia. Burchell's zebra is quite common. Its stripes reach under the belly; then, on the flanks, they broaden and bend backwards towards the rump, forming a Y-shaped saddle pattern. In the Jubba Valley there are maneless zebra. Yet another zebra found in Somalia is the Grevy's zebra. This one has a white belly without stripes. The hindquarters also have no stripes except for the dorsal stripe which bisects them. On the haunches, the stripes from the flanks, rump and hindlegs seem to bend towards each other and join up. The Burchell's zebra can be found on the banks of the River Shabeelle, whilst the Grevy's zebra inhabit the border areas of Somalia and Kenya, south of Kismaayo on the equator.

Lions roam the northern area of Somalia and some are also found in the centre of the country. Many live in the areas between the rivers Jubba and Shabeelle and in the region bordering on Kenya.

The lions are a magnificent sight; they can measure as much as three metres (nine feet) from head to tail. The male lion has a tawny flowing mane, although in parts of Somalia the manes are sometimes black. Lions are notoriously fierce and can climb trees to await their prey. They kill many wildebeest, zebra, waterbuck,

A Burchell's zebra taking leisurely sips from the water hole

kudu, giraffe and buffalo. The lioness does most of the killing but the male always eats first. Lions also eat fruit. The great roar of the lion can be heard by the camel-herders who are always watching over their animals.

The cheetah is one of the fastest runners in the animal world; it has very long, powerful legs. The ground colour of the coat is tawny to light grey with white underparts. Most of the body is covered with closely spaced black spots merging into black rings on the tail. On each side of the face there is a black stripe running from eye to mouth. Cheetahs are found in the north and northeast of Somalia and along the river banks. They can also be seen around the borders of the northeastern part of Ethiopia and in the far south.

Somali birds are very colourful. Bright red, yellow, blue and

A tired lion cub snoozing in a tree. It is hard to believe that he will grow into the tawny-maned king of the beasts

A cheetah dragging away a freshly killed gazelle. Not even a gazelle can outrun this animal, the fastest mammal on earth

green species flit among the acacia trees. The vulturine guinea fowl has distinctive black-and-white neck feathers and a blue breast. These birds may be seen in flocks of as many as two hundred and often run instead of flying. Other birds found in Somalia include the hornbill, and the secretary bird which is white and pale grey above and black below with a crest.

The unusual hoopoe bird is also found in Somalia. It is a pinkish-brown colour with conspicuous black and white bars on the lower back and wings. The tail is black with a white bar at the base. It utters a low three-syllable *hoop-hoop-hoop* call. In the breeding season, the call is accompanied by a fluffing-out of the neck feathers and bowing. The hoopoe feeds on the ground, flying to cover on slow butterfly-like wingbeats. It uses its slender curved bill to probe the soil for larvae, worms, large centipedes and occasionally lizards. In winter it eats antlions and termites.

The hallmark of the hoopoe is its crest of chestnut, black-tipped feathers. Legend has it that hoopoes originally bore crests of gold and this led to their being killed. The hoopoes petitioned King Solomon who was renowned for his wisdom and could understand the language of animals, to ask for divine help. As a result, hoopoes were granted crests of feathers instead of gold. The Somalis also have a legend that King Solomon used to talk to the hoopoe bird and the hoopoe told him when the Queen of Sheba was coming to visit him. Hoopoes appear in many ancient legends; the ancient Egyptians used the hoopoe head in their hieroglyphs (picture writing). The Somalis consider it good fortune to see a hoopoe bird.

The hoopoe. The cry of *hoop-hoop-hoop* and the crest of black-tipped russet feathers are its hallmarks

Modern Somalia: Looking Ahead

Since the revolution, the Somali government has taken over control of all aspects of public life. Strict centralization of power under Siyad Barre's rule has produced many beneficial changes in the country's economy, education and social welfare, although there are many aspects of Somali public life which show the shortcomings of such a system of government.

Since independence, there has been a strong emphasis on the improvement of educational standards. Although education is not compulsory, most Somalis are very keen to learn and since the revolution most of the population have received a basic education. For those who wish to study beyond secondary school, there are colleges for vocational and teacher training. There are two ministries of education: one for primary and secondary education, and the other for higher studies. The National University of Somalia is based in Mogadishu. In addition, many Somali students obtain scholarships to study in universities abroad. In 1985 fifty-seven Somalis were awarded scholarships to British universities alone. Somalia now has an estimated 400,000 students, compared with 40,000 before the revolution. However, the number of graduates has not yet made much impact on primary education, where there are shortages of trained teachers.

Shortages of trained staff affect the Somali health services even more acutely. Although a network of hospitals has been built throughout the country, the wards are usually large and overcrowded, with the exception of some of the more recent buildings in the capital co-funded by various foreign countries including member states of the European Economic Community (EEC) and the Soviet Union. Since few hospitals possess proper canteens or sufficient nursing staff, relatives are expected to provide the patients' food. It is quite common to see members of a patient's family asleep under his or her bed: however unorthodox by medical standards, this practice ensures that the patient is fed and washed regularly.

Malnutrition and poor standards of hygiene combine with the local climate to aid the spread of many dangerous diseases. Malnutrition, caused by deficiencies of diet (eating only one kind of food, or simply not having enough to eat) is particularly harmful to small children. Many of them go on to develop a disease called kwashiorkor (caused by lack of protein in their food) or dysentery (an infectious disease which leads to severe dehydration of the body).

In Somalia, as in so many African countries, much needs to be done to improve the health care system. However, it is a difficult

86

Women waiting outside the village dispensary, where they and their children will receive basic medical attention

task, given the shortage of funds and the recurring periods of famine caused by droughts.

All the Somali media—publishing, newspaper printing, radio and television—are controlled by the state. Newspapers, which are available in all the larger towns, are mainly in the Somali language. There is, however, a weekly English-language edition of *Heegan* ("Vigilance"), while some other papers are available in Arabic and Italian. The name of the Somali News Agency is SONNA.

Somali broadcasting depends largely on the popular transistor radios which are widely available. Radio receivers broadcast public announcements from the government to the remote areas of the country. There are an estimated 95,000 such receivers. Radio Mogadishu and Radio Hargeysa are the two main broadcasting stations.

The radio has helped to unify Somali dialects into a common language, spoken and understood throughout the country. It is very important to Somalis that their language should not become corrupted with foreign words. On occasions, Somali poets have been called in to help find the right phrase in Somali for technical terms from other languages.

Somali language is also used in the newspapers and television broadcasting. Television has been introduced to a limited area with reception within a 30-kilometre (18-mile) radius of Mogadishu. This was financed by Kuwait and the United Arab Emirates. Programmes in Somali and Arabic are transmitted for two hours on Friday, the Muslim day of rest, while on public holidays they continue for three hours. There are plans to build a second transmitter with a wider radius. However, most television sets are located in public buildings in the larger cities, which means that few people have an opportunity to watch television programmes.

The government is aware of the impact of the media on a population keen to have news, entertainment and education. Popular artists from the National Theatre and various arts groups have appeared on radio or television to convey political messages through comedy and song.

Public transport in Somalia suffers from underfunding: there are, for example, no railways, because economic needs elsewhere put railways low on the list of priorities for development. Therefore nearly all the transportation of goods is done by trucks.

Smaller loads are carried by donkeys and camels. The camels are used by nomads to transport their homes, while the donkeys are particularly useful in the cities. They carry large loads patiently and with little cost to their owners. When people move house in town, they load all their possessions onto a wooden platform attached to the donkey's back with ropes. Donkeys carrying milk- and water-cans or firewood are also a common sight.

The quality and availability of passenger transport varies

A water vendor with his donkey-drawn cart. The patient, sturdy donkeys are widely used to transport goods

A street in Mogadishu.
Motor transport is
available in most cities in
Somalia

across Somalia. Mogadishu has an international airport and there are smaller domestic airports at Baidoa and Hargeysa. There are also six airfields scattered around the country. The state-owned Somali Airlines fly frequently to Egypt, Italy, Kenya, Qatar, the United Arab Emirates, Saudi Arabia, Djibouti and the Federal Republic of Germany.

The main seaports are Mogadishu, Berbera and Kismaayo—the old ports of Marka and Baraawe have closed down. Several foreign shipping lines, especially the Italian ones, visit the Somali ports, transporting passengers and goods.

Many people travel by bus and there are regular bus services in all the larger towns. Buses are often crowded and some people have to stand all the way. The red-and-yellow Fiat taxis are a more comfortable, if also more expensive, way of getting about; however, their fares are not as high as those in the West, and some people even go to work in them!

Private car transport, mostly confined to the cities, is as varied and colourful as elsewhere in the world. There is a big demand for landrovers, which are particularly useful when travelling over desert and scrubland. Some Somalis ride motorcycles or ordinary bicycles; however, it must be remembered that in Somalia walking is the traditional means of getting about. Everywhere, even in the blazing sun, the tall Somali men can be seen walking along, with their women and their cattle following behind.

Despite the occasional hardships and frequent discomforts in daily life, the Somalis greatly enjoy their free time. Much of it is spent within the family circle but many people go out to seek entertainment in the theatres, bars, cinemas and stadiums, provided they live in a town large enough to have such things. There are many who not only watch sports events but also take an active part; running and football are particularly popular. Many international football matches are played annually, especially with the neighbouring countries. Crowds in the large stadium in Mogadishu can be heard roaring from quite a distance when their team has scored a goal.

91

Somalia has been a member of the International Athletics Federation since 1959 and its representatives have competed in the Olympic Games on several occasions. In 1987, the Somali athlete Abdi Billeh won the first gold medal for his country at the World Athletic Championships in Rome. However, many Somali sportsmen prefer to compete on behalf of other countries, because training facilities are so much better abroad.

Somalia has friends in both the East and the West. A number of foreign countries have given financial backing to various Somali projects. Of these, China has been the most generous, building a sports stadium, a national theatre, a maternity hospital and a major road into the north of the country. International organizations such as the European Economic Community (EEC) and the World Bank have also helped fund Somalia's development into a modern state.

In 1974 Somalia joined the Arab League and it has since maintained links with other Muslim countries. It is also a member of the United Nations Organization, and hosted a conference of the Organization for African Unity on one occasion. Somalia has also been involved in cultural exchanges with Tanzania, where some 30,000 Somalis live.

Somalia has seen dramatic changes: once a remote outpost governed by sultans, with ancient traditions little known to the outside world; then divided and exploited by the colonial powers, it has only recently become an independent state. It has experienced wars, outbreaks and aftermaths of famine, and

This woman and her two sons are refugees from the troubled frontier area between Somalia and Kenya. Both war and famine have obstructed Somalia's drive towards independence

radical political change. Although poverty still poses a serious problem for the government, ignorance and illiteracy are fast disappearing. It may be many years before the fruits of this period of struggle are seen, but there is a strong sense among the Somalis that their march into the modern world is progressing despite the many odds.

Index

94